W9-DBL-349

THE PACIFIC NORTHWEST POETRY SERIES

LINDA BIERDS, GENERAL EDITOR

THE PACIFIC NORTHWEST POETRY SERIES

2001   John Haines   *For the Century's End*

2002   Suzanne Paola   *The Lives of the Saints*

2003   David Biespiel   *Wild Civility*

2004   Christopher Howell   *Light's Ladder*

2005   Katrina Roberts   *The Quick*

2006   Bruce Beasley   *The Corpse Flower*

2007   Nance Van Winckel   *No Starling*

NO STARLING

POEMS BY NANCE VAN WINCKEL

UNIVERSITY OF WASHINGTON PRESS SEATTLE & LONDON

No Starling, the seventh volume in the Pacific Northwest Poetry Series, is published with the generous support of Cynthia Lovelace Sears.

© 2007 by the University of Washington Press
Printed in the United States of America
Designed by Audrey Seretha Meyer
12 11 10 09 08 07   5 4 3 2 1
First edition 2007

All rights reserved. No part of this publication may be reproduced or transmitted in any form or by any means, electronic or mechanical, including photocopy, recording, or any information storage or retrieval system, without permission in writing from the publisher.

University of Washington Press
P.O. Box 50096, Seattle, WA 98145 U.S.A.
www.washington.edu/uwpress

Library of Congress Cataloging-in-Publication Data

Van Winckel, Nance.
No starling : poems / by Nance Van Winckel. — 1st ed.
p. cm. — (The Pacific Northwest poetry series)
ISBN-13: 978-0-295-98735-4 (alk. paper)
ISBN-10: 0-295-98735-9 (alk. paper)
ISBN-13: 978-0-295-98736-1 (pbk. : alk. paper)
ISBN-10: 0-295-98736-7 (pbk. : alk. paper)
I. Title.
PS3572.A546N62 2007
811'.54—dc22   2007010406

The paper used in this publication is acid-free and 90 percent recycled from at least 50 percent post-consumer waste. It meets the minimum requirements of American National Standard for Information Sciences—Permanence of Paper for Printed Library Materials, ANSI Z39.48–1984.

Epigraph, p. v: The poem by Kozan Ichikyo is from *Japanese Death Poems*, trans. and ed. Yoel Hoffman (Rutland, Vt.: Tuttle Publishing, 1986).

Empty-handed I entered the world,
Barefoot I leave it.
My coming, my going—
Two simple happenings
That got entangled.

—KOZAN ICHIKYO

CONTENTS

I / DOORMAN

Slate *3*

Waking, Working *4*

Mister *5*

We Called Goodbye, but She Was Already Gone *6*

Agape *7*

Black Stitches, Black Knots *8*

Doorman *9*

The New Boys Will Never Love You *11*

In the New Boy's In-Basket *12*

All Asides Aside *13*

White Marginalia *14*

Errata *15*

RE: The Two New Boys *16*

The Rattled Hymn of the Republic *17*

II / MIDDLE, NOWHERE

Before There Was a Road (On the Way to Wilburville) *21*

Middle, Nowhere *23*

Semé and Semaphore *24*

I Am on a Break *26*

Retrograde: Echoes from Earlier Chapters *27*

Passing Through the Shadows of Great Buildings *28*

The Usual *29*

When the Van Broke Down *31*

III / THRESHOLD

Reentry 35

White Brides, White Mistresses 36

Almost an End of Absinthe 37

Verlaine in Prison 38

Simone Weil at the Renault Factory (1935) 39

At Some Point the River Always Veers Away from the Road 40

The Winter Cow 41

Eurydice 42

Our Ladies of Elsewhere 43

You People 44

IV / WE FALL IN BEHIND

We Fall in Behind 49

Fuck It 50

Notes 51

Upriver: Distinctions of *Never* and *Ever* 52

The Ones You Love Are Cold 53

Let Me Remind You You Are Still Under Oath 54

I Talk to the Bread, I Chat with the Dough 56

Breaking Only Little Laws 57

Indiscriminate Kisses 58

Leastways 60

Adieu 61

Hand-Embroidered Mourning Piece
     for Clara Elisabeth Kriebel, 1779 62

Bid Me Be the Bird 63

Acknowledgments 65

About the Poet 67

I / DOORMAN

SLATE

My too-sharp lefts kept making the bundle in back
sluice right. I was driving with the dead Nance
in the truck bed. The gas gauge didn't work
so there was an added worry of running
out of *juice*. Her word. Her word one
windy evening with the carpets
stripped from a floor, which
surprised us as stone—slate
from the quarry we were
headed to now, but Let's first have us
some juice, she'd said, then, barefoot on bare slate.

The truck-bedded Nance, wrapped in her winding sheet,
thuds left, clunks right. I'm sorry about my driving,
sorry about the million lovely pine moths mottled
on my windshield. Thank *God*, here's the quarry,
and there's the high ledge, where, as a girl long
ago, she'd stepped bravely from the white
towel and stared down. Then she'd held her nose
and leapt out into it—this same cool and radiant air.

WAKING, WORKING

I came to on the ground. In my fist
a handful of indestructible earth.
Already then there was this idea
of work. The body moving like a scythe
over its broad gold day. I was alone
in the hot sun. I sat up, then stood up.

Tried to clear from my mind
the unparalleled power of the dream—to stop
and start again . . . further ahead,
already past the poisoned flowers.

Noon sun in the high now.
Near my hand was a trowel
and a little farther off
half a stone fountain.

MISTER

He was what we half expected, bringer
of order to the orchard. Pears by pears, plums
by plums. His mind moves and our bodies stand
and follow. The hoes drag along.

Taking our fear as a given, he'll start a song
at dusk. Merrily, as mirror and echo, we till
and sing. Gone a-rowing. Smoke and fog
on the water, we row we know not where.

In the real river cattle cool off, then step
one by one into starlight. If we reach the last
peach trees, he'll have the lantern lit. On
we go. The hoes' enormous shadows
rise and fall across our small ones.

Smoke fogs the water
and still no shore in the song.

WE CALLED GOODBYE,
BUT SHE WAS ALREADY GONE

You'd think she'd have wished herself
bon voyage or sweet dreams or
at least adios. You'd assume
she'd have gone with a concealed weapon
on her person.

You'd think we'd stop lighting her lamps.

All the while we'd been buying time
she'd been biding it. You'd suppose
we'd have guessed, had some hunch

—or that her shadow would be bleached out
by now . . . her silver bangles silenced.

On her fire-escape a moon's whittled
to gold shavings, gold husks, gold scales.

Her tree shakes loose the purple plums she loved.
You'd think we could bring ourselves
to pick them.
     No. How they dimple,
   dwarf, and rot.
    Now she belongs to us
  the way they
     belong to the wind.

AGAPE

The sum of one's work coming down to a step
into a room and across cracker crumbs
in the carpet and into the glow of TV light
that never goes off, even though the watcher's
quit watching. And then two steps
to climb over her and open the blinds
and call some people it's too late to call,

holding the door when they carry her out
where it's night now, and the TV's
magenta light and tenor sax play up the deep
inner feelings of some deformed but loving
monster—the sort of sweet complexity
which once held her face for hours,

though the face just seen was completely
unheld—a mouth, a well from which
the stultifying emptiness poured. So
surely it's all right to go back inside
and rock awhile in her rocker
as long as the TV's remote remains lost
and the little dog has gone back to sleep.

BLACK STITCHES, BLACK KNOTS

Loosened and then opened by the opiate drops,
she's nowhere now. Wreathed by a lace
collar . . . after the vise of flesh pressed in
and the inner ice-world cracked.

Sundown in a sideview mirror: gone.
The sap-rise and the wonder. Silver
tatting tools, bumpy backbone of the rapids—
gone too. Curled tongue of rock the river rides.

These lengths of language
trailing out of the body
were the last of her
two workers saw as their needles
tugged stitches through a slumped
white jaw. On a shelf, a radio shut down
its quietly burning city within.

                    *   *   *

A bloodless dawn over the workers'
homebound train. In the coach they face
forward, the glitter of icy suburban woods
racing towards them. Forgive them
as they close their eyes. Forgive them
for saying nothing
as everything here recorded
happened.

DOORMAN

Any gentleness confuses him. He wields
scalpels and chisels. He goes in and goes in.
What's inside is harsh, already hardened
so he is too. He resides there, outside
gossip and grammar, outside water
and wind. He never leaves the threshold.

A radio discharges news briefs, updates. Static
and gray dust. He'd prefer to do no damage,
but damage defines him. Incisions
he'll suture later with flesh-colored
threads. He can approximate
any skin, access any code.

A new boy knocks and leaves a sack of food
and goes away—courier sent by the Chancellors
of Change to the City of the Changeless,
where time unfolds and undoes space.
Unstrung moments take up erratic orbits,

and everything opened closes with a wholeness
that can't be cut. No further scrutiny, no
X-ray of the gut. Here congregate
mute witnesses for the witness stand—
but such uncanny candor,
such stark revelations!

He thinks to them he must seem a poor flautist
who's stepped into the subway car to play, softly
and briefly, and unto whom they are now
expected to proffer coins. His cup passes
but they look away. Music bears no
meaning. Their pockets are empty.

THE NEW BOYS WILL NEVER LOVE YOU

Their breaths won't touch your cheek.
You'd think they breathed no breaths.

With the ones they must communicate,
they whistle—like soldiers behind lines.

We'll look into it, they say, but *it*
shows up quartered by crosshairs.

The island of them floats like green smoke
over green tea. Storm wreckage washes up there.

Airports & avenues: off-loading day-old dead
like loaves from a bread truck.

When they slip the sheets off white faces,
no smiles slice the thin lips.

That whistle. It's your answer. If you
hear them, you're as close as one gets.

IN THE NEW BOY'S IN-BASKET

Whatever he wants to touch, he may,
and whenever. The tools dictate a job
that dictates a motion. No one checking.
No one watching. His vertigo on waking.

He calls the job The Nile. He must catch
a bus for The Nile—get off on a messy street,
brave the addict soldiers who never seem cold
in the cold. He's got unreadable lips to read.

His steps echo on the marble stairs. Down.
He parts the reeds. The Nile waits. Hanging
heavy and rank, it belches devoutly, offers
obscene asides on what bloats out and floats up.
He arrives on time to remove red underthings,
wean rigid fingers from diamond rings.

ALL ASIDES ASIDE

No more shocks. No bruises. No intentions. No will. No
      Will I? No *Where am I?* No spaces to stand in
in the rain. No subways, no appointments, no whimpering
      in one's sleep. The dot off its *I*. No I.

No island. No isolate or standing loose inside oneself
      in the outside winds. So long to detox;
hello to redux, to Red River, Red Sea, to a room
      on a barge in a dream.

On the table: a candle and books with print
      too small to read. Out the window an egret
flies into endless black—a huge humility rising
      and falling with her great white wings.

WHITE MARGINALIA

City under snow, a citizenry
  asleep. White top of a cake. White
    itself and only itself. Dress for a bride,
      gown for a girl in God's river.
        She'd liked her cup of port
          on that porch by the sea. Pale
            cheeks a father held between two
              wide palms. Yes, he'd loved her,
                she was a good girl. Days in, days
                  out, her face and so many others
                    slide forth in dark drawers that clang
                      like coins in a tin box. Yes, this one was
                        despised, this one held night upon night.
                          The mountain goat strays high up
                            through a dream—tufts of white
                              wool sloughed off. He'll lose it all
                                come April. That many
                                  dreams. That many nights.
                                    The white a girl never wanted
                                      to be, she is. And everyone
                                        sees, everyone knows.

ERRATA

: chasm where an animal's horn augered in.
: the years' slow unclaiming of toothmarks, of needles
broken off in the no-longer secret knolls of thighs.
He can't see more because he's seen too much:
the body's ciphers, sparks that burned burrows.

And those ankles' rings? What? As if from
shackles? Great boulders of buttocks
with chiseled alphabets, carved epitaphs.
So much sight leaves a seer sightless. Vast
sea of skin with oars cutting through.

Bright belongings and the world's worldliness
too visible against the bone. Nothing over the skin
rhymes with anything under it. Oh, my petit
amours: bees sucking flowers 'til the nectar's all gone.
: two dimples from which the moths sipped light.

RE: THE TWO NEW BOYS

Only one of you may ring the bell and buzz himself
in. The garden will have two smells—gardenia
and old meat. The body you find there must account
for itself. Only one of you may roll his eyes like dice
in a cup. Nothing arresting about the pose, no footprints,
no weapon, nothing suspicious in the blood.

Only one of you can be the suave one, and one
the wistful. If a wrist tires, one may use the electric
scalpel. Peel back the wound's edges. You can both smoke
when the little hand's on five. One of you decide.

Remember, in Bosch's *Hell*, only one
rode unscathed inside the lovely chariot-egg.
Decide soon. One may wear the badly smudged
expression of brave. One may recite The Parable
of the Cave. The bodies glide on ball bearings
from berths in the wall. Six more wait in the hall.

Wrong ID. Wrong X-ray. Wrong sex, wrong
serum, wrong city. The little hand not even
on the same page as five. Only one of you
may be flippant, one change the station, one run
and one shout up the stairs. Right lock,
wrong drawer; right building, wrong floor.

THE RATTLED HYMN OF THE REPUBLIC

Ants dragged themselves to
the corpse. From the corpse.
Crossroads of ribs, mosque
of skull. Ramparts, turrets,
moats. The worksite of the body
opalescent in frostlight.

She was a big one. Manna . . .
an animal grace in the spectral ice.
She was as far west
as they could get in one day
without changing their homes.

The days estimated for dismantling
stretched into months.

Bubble of blood, altar of tooth, and
a black barrage of anti-anatomical
minions. The late night—ungnawed
toe at the end. We're not
much, but we're hard labor
through the wee hours.

Wind. Lingering storm of bones.
The workers changed their homes.
Typhus had trespassed
past the presumed horizon.
Some slack. Some slackers.
They left little behind.

II / MIDDLE, NOWHERE

BEFORE THERE WAS A ROAD
(ON THE WAY TO WILBURVILLE)

In the early extant versions they covered the slopes with sassafras, then gouged their names—with simpler spellings—into slate. So it was said they were founders, not foundlings. They stood garlanded, pouting.

As always, a close-by fog dodged a far-off wind, and the mountain at hand gave way to the mountain ahead.

      *   *   *

Briefly they regretted eating the lost children's breadcrumbs and hurrying off on the high trails—toward summit, horizon, the quasi-infinite up.

In a dog-eared version they're blue-eyed in the underbrush, too shy to kiss. Gradually she, then he, rears up from a vocabulary vacuum. Her plaintive: *Will, oh Will.*

He wears down rock into road, murmuring *brr, brr* in the night chill.

In the woodcut, a trumpeter swan—white cipher at dusk—rises, soars over them, whosoever they are, and wings away for good.

      *   *   *

They poke about the paths.
It's still early in the old life. The willow
that's about to become the tree of Go Fuck Yourself
is still a shady site for sweet, lingering goodbyes.

He and she console themselves. Surely
other children will pass this way
and eat the crumbs of crumbs.

At the far end of glories, which he will later mock
and she will name Morning,
Wilburville loomed. They woke
and came toward it, rounding
the bend we round today—just here
where the stream still hushes
and becomes the river's nuance.

MIDDLE, NOWHERE

Don't argue. This is where we're
stopping. Where we'll snack on
whatever's gleaming in this tree.
What good the sweetness, what use
the flesh, if not to inch us into dream?

Don't answer. Have more. Let
the caption say here we were
lost. Let the chapter tell we found ourselves
or loitered. Nowhere will be mentioned
our sad, right-on-the-money hearts.

Have this very last one then from the highest
branch. Don't fret. Nothing we did here
shall be found in a footnote or penned
with a leafy flourish into Spectacle #12.

SEMÉ AND SEMAPHORE

Quiet people quietly smoking
in doorways—red-tipped lives
going on. Feverish. Forever-ish.

The book of them is slow-going
but you love them, and you go slowly.

        *   *   *

Do-dah, do-dah all around the old
neighborhood. Girls checking into mirrors
like opening new hotel-room doors.

By chapter ten, our girls are professional sitters,
clocked in at the chair factory—a flat rate
to discern smooth, smoother, smoothest.

Stand. Sit. Don't be the odd girl out.

Once they knew why as well as how,
but now *Why* falls like a rock from a star,
atom by atom losing substance.

        *   *   *

The book has a tower and a watchman
flashing messages with a white flag. What speck
on the far black water receives them? It used
to matter: the old grace. Orchestrated
arms. Nuts fell open. Peaches, cherries.

The old grace. Then: an overly pretty
music. Now: no way to change the record.

I AM ON A BREAK

All in a long day's work
I'd been thrice god-blessed
and twice god-damned. I'd been
dimed and quartered, spit at,
ogled and ignored. Now I wanted
just to sit on the curb and read
a newspaper. I was, in that era,
trying to keep tabs on the war
and on the plight of the last
ivory-tusked elephants.

The mime-life was too involved
with the hands. Me in my marble
whites. Me and the screeching
shit-birds. As statue, I was Ms. Finesse
or Madame Rob-You-Blind. All day
I was regaled by the world
with the world. My cigarette
slowly smoked itself
in the stone mouth.

RETROGRADE: ECHOES
FROM EARLIER CHAPTERS

If only the second wish hadn't been squandered
on more wine for the village feast, or the first
on scarlet plumes for the black-eyed dray.

Best wish, last wish: for a cold to crack the gallows
with a weight of ice. At rope's end, the corpse
ticked by slow degrees toward dawn.

She watched the gibbet snap in a red rim of light.
No further grantings. Surely this life's tasks
end well when the next life's begin.

Morning's too-lateness. Her pipe empty, and no smoke
to warn the villagers of her dreams' demise. If only
she could set back the hours, the days. Before

The Feast. Before Adam or Eden, before love
and animals and small green lands spit up by the sea.
Without one's wishes, what dangles reverts to plain type.

Pages flutter and whisk away the dead. In the chill
of his shadow came a wind, then the pendulum's *tick* . . .
tick . . . *tick*—that word again. How we scorn the redundant.

PASSING THROUGH THE SHADOWS
OF GREAT BUILDINGS

The beggar in plaid blankets wanted to kiss my hand
when it lowered the shiny franc. His eyes sleepy, pleading.

How long would I stand there considering . . . the metal
warming, the light waning. My hand dangling . . . .

THE USUAL

After we'd walked through an abandoned house in the woods and
seen the crows arranged like black hats on a shelf. And after their
shrieks made our hands jerk back from a beggar's bowl, we saw
the snake. All tongue and ire, he blazed up from an old stove. He
fumed like a prophet bearing indictments. We stood stock still.
Around us: the entrail colors of a semi-halted sundown.

*   *   *

Later, resting from the hike, I thought how
    the sweet moths rush off—perhaps sensing
        gold light under a dreamer's door. And ah,
to flit through, to work oneself in there. Not
    being wary. Not suspecting Nabokov
        at the possible center. Doing the
            usual: pushing pins into plush
velvety wings. Licking the powder from
    his fingers: late hours and the verdant eyes
        of iridescent wings wide open. Through
            them, through him, we come to admire
                a girl on page twelve of her waking . . .
                    as she blinks and swats a moth out of a nap.

*   *   *

And so I nod awake as you come by
    and squeeze my hand and say you'd give a rib
        for a beast like me who speaks

            your lingo. I say
         me too. I say blah-blah
      about the moths—what brave journeys
   they make between teacups.

WHEN THE VAN BROKE DOWN

I was on a cliff road, chilled but happy looking down at the sea.
The night stars appeared so new and the van so old—so old
everything seemed to flow from it, even the snaking-out-of-sight blacktop

and the primal tidal clawing at the cliff. So old and so red and broken,
and me as a ruptured part thunked loose on the road.

The breakdown had been rushing toward itself for 200,000 miles,
and it had been waiting patiently for some less sinister century
to materialize right here, where twilight lay tendering in a bed of oil.

The twelfth bolt drops like the last disciple. And surely repair begins
with fresh lipstick applied in the side mirror, where the breakdown

aims to loom larger, be bloodier, spill more guts. It commands quiet.
It wants no one to slow and gawk, no apparition to offer aid, no dog
to sniff or trooper to stop. And no way anyway we'll attract our kind.

This van, this night—we *have* no kind. We scatter handouts to the gulls
who've gathered to gloat, and no doubt our cache only seems so boundless
because our journey was meant to be a long one.

III / THRESHOLD

REENTRY

I was playing again on the stone stairs.
     I could hear the hiss of seconds passing.
       My mother sat as I'd left her,
   among mothers, aiming a thread
through a needle's eye. All was
     as it should be. I shouted grave orders
       to the dolls, my prisoners.
Clearly I was still afraid of my largeness,
    my separateness, my long
horrible arms striking out.

          *   *   *

Supplicants and prey. The hissing
    sweeping hand. All was as it
      ever is. I turned on a top stair.
Open the door, and the world's silver wires
     sizzle—long lit hallways with workers
       hawking their nations' wares.

A passing-by of shoes with gold buttons. So like
     my own. I step over the threshold . . .
      a hissing sweep of my gown.
I open my eyes. Trust now:
    the body will know what I am
      and what to do about it.

WHITE BRIDES, WHITE MISTRESSES

Fog freezing to the greenery, then a skiff
of snow—clouds that will crumble later
as the snow leopard slips into a boy's
dreaming. Neither the boy nor the animal
knows of the dream. Their fear of each other
doubles their beauty. Their desire stills footfalls
and cloaks deep paw prints.

The leopard's eyes do not close
when she's caressed. But they do
when she's kissed—the kiss is so new.

The boy's arms catch in the snowy pelt
with its surprise of warmth
deeper in. *These are my fingers,* the boy
says, *these are my lips.* He senses
the small thing he is when he enters her,
clinging to her haunches,
knowing she feels him barely.

The pressures of her hungers tighten.
His whispers, her quivers—
these swirl a blizzard about them.

The depths she desires press in on him.
The road there is lit like the first dawn,
and the distance clear: high jagged peaks!
White irises, bridges of ice.

ALMOST AN END OF ABSINTHE

Until he's unbitten its bitterness
with sugar in a spoon, with summer
dusk, a ghost light, and the ice's

finger of death—it sits, hollowing
its hole in the table like a burn. He's
its ash, a bud of char on a chair.

       *   *   *

What is real here, the green wonders:
the glass, or the gut full of bile.
It shines a leafy light to see down.

It sips from itself to remember
the wormwood it was taken from
like a man twisted out of a woman's rib.

       *   *   *

A spider climbs into the glass. There
every limb is loved. The legs churn
a white cloud across an emerald expanse.

A milky belljar slips over the slag
of a man who resembles the tip
of a tail—a swish and a shine.

Shot free of its wide unblinking eye,
the green toasts its bright life
and drinks back its death.

VERLAINE IN PRISON

He tells the deputies he was drowned as a boy in a well of holy water,
and so has returned this way: full wet, a rattle of bones beneath his
clothes, and all manner of love for his fellow man coming over him

the way a storm comes over a mountain. The long raucous rain
around them. Boats of stone, hulls sunk deeper in the river.

Badges and fastidious whispers outside the cell: saying an illness
drips out through the blood, saying the sorriest dying kills even the
leeches.

Hours before the Angelus, a storm lights up the vast fearsome space
where two men rock on a bed which rocks them back—all night
taking turns being water, being shore.

SIMONE WEIL AT THE
RENAULT FACTORY (1935)

A thread in a line of threads, she stands
at the far end of herself. Eyelets and inlets,
divots for ingots. Migraines are the grain
of the day. In the awl's hollows, the nothing
God is to teach us the nothing we are.

The coupe is a cave. Go in and kneel
on its seat. Hands tool the tools
without us: to work to eat; to eat to work.

Where are the streets for such vehicles? Not yet
made. Where's the fuel to make go Go?
Underground, still pressing itself to become itself.

Punched-in lead holes; the head aches
when it's emptied out. A cold outside
comes in. The coupe is a cave.
Shine its horn; buff its blast.

The cave wheels forth—God,
where is it going? Into more rat-a-tat-
tat. More hands, less us; more air
in the airguns, less loud the heart.

AT SOME POINT THE RIVER ALWAYS VEERS AWAY FROM THE ROAD

Like all machines, this one hums in B flat.
Wired into it, a girl thinks of paddling a small
yellow boat, of important checks and balances
on the burgeoning rapids. Room E, Floor 12, Ward

of the Moon. Inside, the sound of blood-slosh
into steel. She's in the closed eye that hits the white froth
and spins like a top. Sweet the yellow blur. Sweet
the swirled rock cliffs, the sun's red roar.

She rights the boat. Only for a few more miles
do the road's curves follow the narrowing river's.

THE WINTER COW

The cow stood to be milked. She had to.
She had to last until May since the milk
was needed. All four hooves had been sawed off
exactly five inches up, cauterized, and cleaned
with a fresh cloth daily. The freeze in the field
had been extreme and unexpected in November.

The boy sat with his bucket beneath her
like someone alive in the mists of the underworld.
Extra hay for her on Wednesdays and Saturdays.
Careful, careful: the slightest tap could topple her.

Her smell was of raw earth and the grain
that spins in her sinuous turbines,
then falls as a white froth at one's feet.

He'd tried to sing a few songs for her
but there wasn't one that didn't crack
like a stick in his throat. He hummed.

The body is a great boat that knows the way
through iced blue distances. Gravity's small hands
tug at the hull. You get in
and you close your eyes, and you go.

EURYDICE

She knew the coolness far down
and years back had buried her dolls
in sand. First she'd dressed them
in silk gowns. Hours coiling their ornate
coiffures. They would never be asked
to answer any summons to ascend—only hear,
steadily overhead, the sea
pouring back and forth.

After this interment, she was herself
unclear about routes home: via remote
bird calls and beckonings. Each toe
felt new as she crept through the surf.

The earth pressed down: gold, tender.
The dreamers' impenetrable warmth
inside an inviolate cold. They slept
in sand like rain in the treetops.

Their dreaming made her fearless.
Their clear fates settled their faces
into No Expectations. Their hardness
softened hers and made her venture
a step higher on the unfamiliar stairs.

OUR LADIES OF ELSEWHERE

They douse the burning bush. They count
   the world's money. Each in her own way, in her
      own time. And if they walk in beauty, it's
         because they're mindless of it—so we
           may be mindful. Dear me, dear you,
        the *Daily* flies out from the dark
     and bangs at the door, and they're
  in that too—peeping between pixels
in the thousand-dots-an-inch train wreck.

One's calamities incite their yawns and sighs.
   They burp and sneer over beautiful miseries
      at the end of ecstasies. What blister on the heart
         don't we get? What callings from the trees don't
           we hear? One's sweet obsession they sip away
        in the worst god-awful wine, then curtsy
     and leave us the lees. And here, just here where
  the loud stream pivots and enters the silent river,
how dare they swim you now, white frill?

YOU PEOPLE

People, don't ask me again where my shoes are.
The valley I walked through was frozen to me
as I was to it. My heavy hide, my zinc
talisman—I'm fine, people. Don't stare
at my feet. And don't flash the sign of the cross
in my face. I carry the Blue Cross Card—
card among cards, card of my number
and gold seal. So shall ye know I am of
the system, in the beast's belly and up
to here, people, with your pity.

People, what is wrong with you? I don't care
what the sign on your door says. I will go
to another door. I will knock and rattle
and if *you* won't, then surely someone, somewhere,
will put a pancake in my hand.

You people of the rhetorical *huh*? You lords and ladies
of the blooming stump, I bend over you, taste you,
keep an eye on you, dream for you the beginning
of what you may one day dream an end to.

The new century peeled me bone-bare
like a song inside a warbler—that bird, people,
who knows not to go where the sky's stopped.
Keep this in mind. Do you think

the fox won't find your nest? That
the egg of you will endure the famine?

You, you people born of moons with no
mother-planets, you who are back-lit,
who have no fathers in heaven, hear now
the bruise-knuckled knock of me. I am returned.

From your alley. From your car up on blocks.
From the battered, graffitied railcars that uncouple
and move out into the studded green lightning.

Do you believe because your youth's
been ransacked, nothing more will be asked of you?
And people, about the shoes: the shoes
have no doubt entered the sea and are by now
walking the ramparts of Atlantis.
I may be a false prophet, but god bless me, at least
I have something to say. Supine in a pencil of night,
I've no chiseled tip yet, but already
the marks take form in the lead.

IV / WE FALL IN BEHIND

WE FALL IN BEHIND

The Line Starts Here. You take a ticket
and wait. The Line wends through chasms,
gulleys, fissures. Between boxed-up provisions
of fruit and flowers. You have many lives
and while one may be for speedy departures
and another for false arrivals, one is always for
The Line, for taking a turn singing . . .
something without gist or consequence.

Watch the big man when he's called. The Line
coughs him forward. His proud belly juts
ahead. He passes through the arch of questions
into salt air, breezes, and more questions. We fall in
behind—in step and on time. It's
the nature of the beast that is The Line
to make us believe in *wait* . . . crumpets
proffered on a crystal plate. The Line keeps us
going where it goes, arriving
where it's been. The Line costs us, ages us,
leads us up from the underworld
and one day straight back in.

FUCK IT

A mist obscures the smoke
that's obscured the fire, and my sense
of having been set down like a satchel
on a crumbling step. My straps
unstrapped. The song in my head
over. When the song had said *drift*,
I'd drifted. When it said *Take out your heart
and eat,* I took. I ate. I swore
I could distinguish the Everlasting
from the Eternal—by that little blip of bliss
in the latter, and surely it shone.

I was in the last seconds of a last try
        on a last poem, and they too
            would pass. A window opens.
Fugue moment. Moment of needing
        the formerly shunned world. Also
            passing. Also past. If I'd been wrong
                about the smoke, I'd be
                    wrong about the fire.

NOTES

An uncorked something red, a slow dream,
and the serving girl saying she's only
telling me what she's been told to: take
my notes if I must, but take them out back.

In my absence, the ciphers and smooth destinies
of saxophone and drum roll on.

Here comes the trick of light
through the trees. Foothills, old
familiars, I enter you from due east.
Swaybacks, saw-tooth and gap-
mouthed, I take note. Hunched over.
A thing on a step to step over.

Tricked-out light. Watch out. Bone.
Bone-quiet.
Bone ash, bone dust.

UPRIVER: DISTINCTIONS
OF *NEVER* AND *EVER*

A tall man in a robe keeps the godly people
waiting near the river. They've staked big tents
and tiny poodles, and they've dunked one another
so they have some clue about the water's cold.

The heron glides right on
over them. Crazy atop the crazier thermals,
she's been spitting down fish bones.
She's a weight the air can hold.

When the robed one steps into the rushing
water, a few wail in what may be joy. Hard
to know. We paddle by. Today's sunrise
seems more a broken than a breaking thing.

Upriver, the elk step out and sip at something
the old sheep—thirsty as they are—would never drink.

THE ONES YOU LOVE ARE COLD

Shut in with matches. Shut up with cigars
and quarters in their caskets. Calla lilies
you know they'd mock. Shut down
with both eyes open, with ongoing prayers
for the President. Sent off without Scotch
or Sanka or the pretty pink cough syrup.

No black phone or red penknife. No maps. But
a Bible, a missal. Five rosaries, four holy cards.

You know what they whisper and don't care
who hears: our misplaced wickets, misplayed trump.
Their too-long hair. Broken chokers of pearls. Thin
air. Long toenails, crumbling thresholds . . .

They want August. The back alley's clatter.
September sun. They want to sit up. Drink
warm milk and deal from a fresh deck. They wish
we'd quit with these lists and come find them.

LET ME REMIND YOU
YOU ARE STILL UNDER OATH

Out of marsh out of the bronchial
treelimbs out of low clouds
we grow up to be President, we emerge
as nurses or greengrocers or red lips
waiting for a cigarette. From the lagoon
beside the postcard meadow under elk-
antlered skies we are raised to a flame
in a streetlight. Arterial dust mites.
A gnat's death banged out by the *NY Times*.

From the Why-hast-thou
and the We'll-be-back-soon, through
siren wail and bird call
we step up with our sticks
and stigmatas, our forged
documents. We mature
into the foxtrot and cha-cha-cha.

Past the *Dead End* and *Deaf Child* signs
and out of the valley's huge cowbells
we evolve as hammers chisels
sprung traps. We ring up the Colonels of Parks
who call friends who've just dredged
the Erie Canal and are en route
to zip open Panama but can meet us

for a moment with our paper sacks
and pitchforks. They accept our potatoes.

From woodlands. From bobcat bellies. Over
downed fences. Out of ashes and owl eyes shining
we are passed on with a B- by new boys in plaid kilts.

The unhinged eye of the compass spins
and we migrate: first fern, first night's first dream
the first fathers suffered: a flower expelling its seed.

We step over the wires, and still keeping taut
the thread of a hard-hearted folksong, we arrive
at an age to shoot the last crows
off the slumped barn. We're the Presidents
the Colonels have called
and our voices shouting *What? What?*
fill the forest of felled trees.

I TALK TO THE BREAD,
I CHAT WITH THE DOUGH

I say rise and it sits.
I hum sweetly
but it sours. I say for
the living, for the love of,
the sitteth on the right hand of.

I say s'il vous plait
and pass through the room
flashing my girl-sized, old-lady
breasts. At least
and why not for the gumbo—
a soup to circulate
in the soap bubble of the world.

Our world. C'est moi. May
not another thing happen out there
as nothing happens endlessly
in here. C'est tu. Say no more turning
our respective backs
to the rain. Tell me sit
and I will rise again.

BREAKING ONLY LITTLE LAWS

Might you say, do you think—if
     you were me, would I pick
          those kids up, take them
               to Tennessee? Mightn't I, as you,
          share the map? Last smoke in the pack?
     Imagine I can get, thank-god, to the end
of a joke. Imagine I'm nicer
     than you've known me, and see—
          I offer salsa and don't even lick
               the someone else's bowl. I'm wanting
          honest input. Would I answer the kids
     about when, for how long, or if
the storm terror of childhood
     ever shuts down? Might I say we crawl
          out of the inland sea and fly up
               in the way of the geese, taking turns
          at the head of the V? Wouldn't you, i.e., me,
     turn off on Tra-la-la Lane
and toss a bra in the backseat? Kiss
     once to get the strangeness out?
          Twice to seal the deal? Think
               please. Think a minute
                    and just say yea or nay.

INDISCRIMINATE KISSES

Foreplay of obscene graffiti carved
into trees—foot-long boners
gouge the bark. Beaks and snouts
on a restroom mirror. Slick lips.
Succulent lips. I go out among them
sometimes. So sweet how they pucker up
out of pity. A practiced pathos
in a saloon of woodsmen whose axes
wait in trucks out back. Lips full of yawn
or yes. Lips thick with God-spit
and God-suck. Chapped lips, bloody lips.
Pierced or tattooed, they pout
into view—here to give, willy-nilly,
what's been too-long held in the body.
Something passes across tongues. It sayeth not
a name; it taketh everyone's turn. Mute lips
of a swift unbuttoner. Mouths fording
frothy streams, vaporous bogs.
I stumble forth in their midst. Maybe
I am out of bread or in a bad place
with a book. The streets have an attendant
caress. Moon lapping rumor. Fat lip
approaches harelip. There go pasty
lips. All are readied as if for a race
or to be plucked like rare moths

by bright wings from the air. Betty's lips
and Bobby's and Bucky's just before the collision
and the siren's red wail. Laddy, keep
a light on. I may have to come ashore
some distance from where I set in.

LEASTWAYS

The ship had a bar, listing. A porthole
awash. Loyal drinkers swearing they'd seen
the giant squid. Sheer genius, they said,
to survive the millennia, the depths.

I blinked into that window at only
my face . . . all splash and dissolve.

Days under the white sails, over
cruel swells. Days taken
like aspirin. Hard little fact
of the body: if *it* goes down,
I go. And the bar raised. The bar
tilted. A tentacled here-on portends
a hereafter. I hang on. Rain clouds
pretend to take the lead.

ADIEU

A woman knelt to drink from the river,
  and dipping cupped hands saw the face
    that had been hurried through the woods
      all day. A twig and a leaf in the blown-
        back hair. Bending, drinking, she watched
          the face travel down the river. More easily
satiated, it had finished sipping sooner.
  Passing along ripples, it closed
    its eyes. There seemed to be laughter
      as it swirled around a rock and an *Oh!*
      as it bobbed past a log. Transported
        among trout and dragonfly, it went green
under the greenery, then grew calm,
  though less distinct, as it drifted into the flat
    middle of the river, where water hoarded
      the little that was left of sunlight. It never
        glanced back at the one still kneeling, still
          recalling the cool wet kiss of parting.

HAND-EMBROIDERED MOURNING PIECE
FOR CLARA ELISABETH KRIEBEL, 1779

Nobody outsang her, nobody outswam her. Blue
water. Blue silences. Nobody crossed the bay
before her. No one outshot her, took deeper
breaths. Sang higher, harder, longer.

Once her bullets flew so fast she didn't have time
to aim. Once she cut up and skinned two
huge beasts between sunup and sunset,
and a very short cold day it had been.

No one had less fear of the lakebed's muck
or of the silver tools that pry open the rib bars
around a delicious heart. Even the blood soup
was superb: a muscle of sea inside it.

No one out-ate her, was lovelier, or happier
alone. Once the willow in her yard was smaller
than this one by her gravestone. Not a soul
outclimbed her. No one outguessed her.
Here she still runs forward—farthest,
fastest. Now no one outsleeps her.

BID ME BE THE BIRD

May the bluer tidal flux of the world
stop belonging to me. May it quit lapping
at my feet. I've emerged from the mine.
I've flown a branch quite far in my beak.

When I began these documents, they faced
forward: their end in the distance.
Now that distance is tilled rye fields—there
a great beast with a hundred other beasts
in its belly. May what they stew on be stirred.

I've got wings is the point. The soul's central issues
are dizzying, and I am a slave to them, as they are
to the Fill-in-the-Blank, or the dot, dot, dot.

I know the way to the mouth. I flap along
amid ambitious bodyguards of clouds—none
with any clout. I pick up and put down
the stick. May the brotherhood of scattered limbs
one day be returned to the olive tree.

Of a dark, diluvian night, sometimes
a beast tries to flee the field. Steady wings
steady the point, dynasties of meaning set in motion.

Mouth, mouth: my light
and my exit. Let nothing block
the route. Good tidings. Green sightings.
I wish all of your houses well.

ACKNOWLEDGMENTS

*Thanks to the editors of these journals for first publishing
    the following poems:*

AGNI: "Slate," "Adieu," "Reentry," "Eurydice," and "Waking Working"
American Literary Review: "The New Boys Will Never Love You"
American Poetry Review: "Agape," "Black Stitches, Black Knots,"
    "Leastways," "Fuck It," and "Notes"
Ascent: "Upriver: Distinctions of *Never* and *Ever*"
Colorado Review: "RE: The Two New Boys" and "Doorman"
Denver Quarterly: "Errata"
Field: "Semé and Semaphore"
Gettysburg Review: "The Winter Cow" and "When the Van Broke Down"
Idaho Review: "In the New Boy's In-Basket"
Indiana Review: "Almost an End of Absinthe"
Kenyon Review: "Let Me Remind You You are Still Under Oath"
Laurel Review: "Our Ladies of Elsewhere"
New England Review: "Simone Weil at the Renault Factory"
New Letters: "Retrograde: Echoes from an Earlier Chapter," "The Ones
    You Love Are Cold," "Passing Through the Shadows of Great Build-
    ings," and "Bid Me Be the Bird"
Ninth Letter: "Mister"
Ploughshares: "Verlaine in Prison"
Poetry: "At Some Point the River Always Veers Away from the Road,"
    "Indiscriminate Kisses," "Hand-Embroidered Mourning Piece for
    Clara Elisabeth Kriebel, 1779," and "You People"
Poetry East: "All Asides Aside"
Poetry Northwest: "I Am on a Break"
Southern Review: "Middle, Nowhere"

"Let Me Remind You You are Still Under Oath" is in *Red, White, & Blues: Poetic Vistas on the Promise of America* (U. of Iowa Press). "You People" appears in *The Pushcart Prize Anthology XXX*; "You People" and "Simone Weil in the Renault Factory" appear in *Long Journey: Contemporary Northwest Poets* (Oregon State University Press, 2006).

Thanks also to the National Endowment for the Arts for a 2001 Poetry Fellowship, which helped toward the completion of this collection.

ABOUT THE POET

Nance Van Winckel teaches in the graduate creative writing programs at Eastern Washington University and Vermont College. She is the author of four books of poetry (*Bad Girl, with Hawk*, 1987; *The Dirt*, 1994; *After a Spell*, 1998; and *Beside Ourselves*, 2004) and three collections of short stories, and she publishes regularly in *American Poetry Review, Ploughshares, AGNI, The Gettysburg Review*, and other journals. Her numerous awards include two National Endowment for the Arts Poetry Fellowships, a Pushcart Prize, two Washington State Artist Trust Awards, and *Poetry Magazine*'s Friends of Literature Award. *After a Spell* received the Washington State Governor's Award for Poetry.